One Way to Teach the Writing of Poetry

Christy Barnes

Printed with support from the Waldorf Curriculum Fund

Published by:

Waldorf Publications at the
Research Institute for Waldorf Education
38 Main Street
Chatham, NY 12037

Title: *One Way to Teach the Writing of Poetry*
Author: Christy Barnes
Layout: Ann Erwin
Cover image: Richard Zippel sketch made during Ms. Barnes' History of Poetry block at the Rudolf Steiner School, New York

ISBN 978-1-943582-04-4
A large part of this essay is reprinted here with kind permission from *Renewal: A Journal for Waldorf Education*, Fall/Winter 1993, with a few additions and changes made by the author.

One Way to Teach the Writing of Poetry

Students graduating from the twelfth grade carry with them, one hopes, a sense of the world's poetry from ancient times up to the present. This sense grows with them daily and monthly from kindergarten on. But there is a magical opportunity in which the teacher has the creative freedom to concentrate on poetry's most essential elements. This is in the tenth grade of a Waldorf school's "History of Poetry" block.

During this block, each morning for half or three quarters of an hour, the students can drink in the nature of poetry through the spoken word as they practice a poem in chorus and then listen to one another speak self-chosen verses from a group of poems selected by the teacher. Soon they have absorbed from each other much more than their own assignment. Some are eager to pass off their poems quickly; others need more time. Helped by this situation, the teacher can, without too much trouble, foster an atmosphere of lively volunteering. It is, of course, the poems the children learn earliest, in the elementary school, which stay with them the longest.

A good teacher will provide the children through the years with a substantial but varied diet: enough salty ballads, a scattering of peppery verses, poems with beauty to give the children vision, and poems with "iron" and substance enough to make their souls sturdy, build them a backbone, and give them little chance of becoming undernourished and anemic in spirit.

But poems assigned the children as pieces of educational baggage or as specimens only to be analyzed will lie within them undigested, ready to be spewed forth on a test and soon gratefully forgotten. Poems, like loaves of bread, need to be baked through by the voice, enthusiasm and experience of the teacher. Then they can be taken up "by heart" by the students and circulated through their whole being to become a permanent part of themselves. This fund of poetry, living in the subconscious, gives the children a general sense of wealth and health. And it may be drawn up to consciousness from time to time for inspiration, pleasure, consolation—or as a measuring stick against which to evaluate new poems, experiences and perplexities.

The images that have given color, drama, humor and joy in the elementary school can become something more to tenth-grade adolescents. As their inner life deepens and opens out, they are ready to grasp the conception that the sun, a star, the human eye, the face of a daisy, a luminous thought are all inhabited and imbued by the same out-radiating principle: invisible to the physical eye but clearly apprehended by the inner, unseen eye of the soul—an eye that can see through to the unifying principle that creates analogy after analogy. This inner eye the poets have named *imagination.*

Through its lens we can look, for instance, into the realm of time, into the no-longer-visible past, and visualize the causes that have led to our present deeds and situation. Learning from these, we can penetrate into the not-yet-seeable future—hopefully in time to adjust and amend our plans to more beneficial and less disastrous ends.

The poet sees the most potent characteristics of his own times and depicts these for us, sometimes with an almost mirror-like faithfulness. But he is also one of the first to see, as from a watch-tower, the dawn of a coming age and help to reflect the light of its influence into the present world.

The great literature of the world fills our imagination with the joys, sufferings, customs, religions and aspirations of people very different from ourselves. Our understanding widens, our judgment matures, our compassion deepens.

If we look with the eye of imagination deeply enough into the nature of a Buddhist, a Hebrew, a Christian, of a Russian, a Chinese, Serbian or a Croat, what do we discover? In the inmost center of each, we see a human being like ourselves. All persons of all races, nations and creeds upon our entire globe are united by their native humanity, by their common destiny. Once assured of this kinship, we can become free to welcome, explore and enjoy the infinite variety in which this single universal fact expresses itself. Must we forever concentrate on the inconveniences of our differences instead of drawing pleasure from the wealth of our diversity? Must all gardens be planted with one kind of flower only? Shelley tells us in his *Defense of Poetry* that:

> The great instrument of moral good is imagination;
> poetry strengthens the faculty which is the organ
> of the moral life of man in the same way as exercise
> strengthens a limb.

There is nothing so demoralizing as to live in a world without meaning. But each new analogy—and analogy is a great part of the power of poetry—each analogy reveals unifying harmonies in the world around us and makes life meaningful. This meaningfulness can satisfy one of our deepest longings and fill us with relief, purpose and zest for life.

In poetry, imagination is carried by the dancing feet of rhythm, the melody of vowels and the sculpture and motion of consonants. These can move the listener to joy or melancholy, to a war-like or a gentle mood. Great music can give our feelings a finer, fuller, more compassionate strength—unless the heart is too hardened or inert to respond to it.

Poetry and music can become a powerful counterforce to dullness and untrustworthiness. Prose conveys imagery, but a poem is a thought become imagery and music. Poets and scientists alike have recognized that music works as a powerful harmonizing force in both nature and in man.

Thomas Carlyle wrote: "All things are song. Poetry is musical thought. See deep enough and you see musically, the heart of nature being everywhere music, if you can only reach it." And in Shelley's lyrical drama *Prometheus Unbound* we find this poem:

> He gave man speech
> and speech created thought
> which is the measure of the universe;
>
> And the harmonious mind
> poured itself forth in all
> prophetic song.
>
> And music lifted up
> the listening spirit
> until it walked—
> exempt from mortal care,
> god-like
> o'er the clear billows
> of sweet sound.

The high school boys and girls learn how to scan these "clear billows." They learn about rhyme, alliteration and figures of speech. They learn also about the subtleties of tone color, which is the more varied and informal repetition of sounds occurring—not regularly as do rhyme and alliteration—but unpredictably anywhere within stanzas.

At the time of the Battle of Hastings in 1066, two powerful streams of culture and language met, like the meeting of two vast rivers, and battled against each other. The southern stream won, lived on in castles, and ate *beef.* The northern, Anglo-Saxon stream waited upon their victors and tended their *cows.* The Norman stream loved the lilt of rhyme (*singing, winging*) and the musical, dancing exchange of long and short syllables. The Anglo-Saxons smote their words as they smote trees with axes and table-boards with beer mugs. With the southern stream it was the length of the syllable that counted; with the northern, it was the weight—let the short syllables fly up into the wind at will. Usually of the four, heavy, stressed syllables in each line, three of them began with the same consonant. Theirs was alliterative verse. Gradually the two cultures intermingled and, as a token of this enriching friendship, we have the captivating little round combining Anglo-Saxon vocabulary with rhyme and length, not weight of syllables:

CUCKOO SONG

Sumer is icumen in
  Lhude sing cuccu!
Groweth sed, and bloweth med,
  And sprigth the wude nu—
      Sing cuccu!

Awe bleteth after lomb,
Lhouth after calve cu;
Bulluc sterteth, bucke verteth,
Murie sing cuccu!

Cuccu, cuccu, well singes thu, cuccu:
Ne swike thu naver nu;
Sing cuccu, nu, sing cuccu,
Sing cuccu, sing cuccu, nu! c. 1250 AD

The class should already be familiar with the nature of the five meters or rhythms which poets have used for the last twenty centuries or so, and know that rhyme was not used until the 4th century AD when it was first used by Christian monks in North Africa. Before that, poetic form in the southern stream of literature depended upon varied meters of which the ancient Greeks used twenty-four. I have never had deeper or more relaxed attention from a class as when I read them all of these, one after the other, simply saying: "long, long, short, long; long, long, short, long; — short, long, short, short; short, long, short, short," holding each syllable for the proper length of time.

Twenty-four Ancient Greek Meters

Meters Still Used Commonly Today

Iambus	⏑ –	to throw; assertive, rising rhythm
Trochee	– ⏑	to run; story-telling, falling rhythm
Dactyl	– ⏑ ⏑	finger; harmonious, healing, solemn
Anapest	⏑ ⏑ –	turned back on itself; dancing, lively
Spondee	– –	to pour a libation to the gods

Meters Seldom Used Today

Pyrrhichius	⏑ ⏑	fiery
Tribrachus	⏑ ⏑ ⏑	three shorts
Molossus	– – –	used in Tennyson's "Break, break, break"
Amphibrach	⏑ – ⏑	
Bacchius	⏑ – –	
Antibacchius	– – ⏑	
Amphimacer	– ⏑ –	
Antispast	⏑ – – ⏑	
Choriambus	– ⏑ ⏑ –	
Jonicus I	⏑ ⏑ – –	used in "Seafever" by Masefield
Jonicus II	– – ⏑ ⏑	
Epitritus I	⏑ – – –	
Epitritus II	– ⏑ – –	
Epitritus III	– – ⏑ –	
Epitritus IV	– – – ⏑	used in "Seafever"
Paeon I	– ⏑ ⏑ ⏑	
Paeon II	⏑ – ⏑ ⏑	
Paeon III	⏑ ⏑ – ⏑	
Paeon IV	⏑ ⏑ ⏑ –	

Line Length

one foot	–	one verse
two feet	–	dimeter
three feet	–	trimeter
four feet	–	tetrameter
five feet	–	pentameter
six feet	–	hexameter
seven feet	–	heptameter

But how do we teach students to write poetry as we teach them to paint or make music? How do we teach them to write their own poems? Do we assign them a theme or do we lead them into the music and sculpture of language? Do we say, "Write me a poem about snow"? Or do we perhaps write on the blackboard:

> Along the long, low line of the lonely hills
> The snow fell soft and…

and say, "Now go on from there." Perhaps the whole class tries to do this together right then, orally, or you tell them each to make up a line filled with beautiful or powerful sounds and go on to write for homework a four-line poem with a regular rhythm and rhyme scheme—perhaps:

˘ – ˘ – ˘ – ˘ – **a**
˘ – ˘ – ˘ – **b**
˘ – ˘ – ˘ – ˘ – **a**
˘ – ˘ – ˘ – **b**

No one can really teach poetry unless he makes poetry himself, throws himself head over heels into the waters of language and learns to swim in its rhythm, music and flow. This swimming comes to its full glory with revision and rewriting: choosing just the right word, avoiding any unnatural word order, tuning and matching the sounds, shading and heightening the gloom or the glow, awakening a whole bee-swarm of rhymes, each suggesting a new image or idea, then weeding away the weaker ones. We must be sure that we have at last fished up and landed the unifying conception that we have all along been trying to catch—a thought so alive and dripping with imagery and tone that, as Carlyle says, it is itself music.

During the next days read to them the various poetic forms which follow here, and have them each write a poem in all or most of these forms. Do this before you have them write in free verse. Free verse does not have, of itself, the restrictive demands that exercise and strengthen the muscles that give form and force to a poem. It can, though, have both if the writer has already learned these by wrestling with the demands of strict forms, or, of course, if he or she is very gifted.

Anglo-Saxon Verse Form

In Anglo-Saxon verse each line has four stresses, three of which usually begin with the same sound.

BEOWULF

original

Hwät! we Gar-Dena   in geär-dagum
theod cyninga   thrym gefrunon
hu tha aðhelingas*   ellen fremedon

word-for-word translation

What! we Spear Danes   in yore-days
warrior kings   power seized
from the noblemen   brave splendidly

translation

Listen! how   on days of yore
we Spear Danes   seized power
from noblemen   splendidly brave.

*ð is the Old English letter for *th* as pronounced in *thing*.

AUTUMN BIRCH

Glad and gold   are the blazing birch-blossoms,
Lemon-leaves shining   above the white earth mother,
Tossed by storm-serpents   slashed by hail stones,
Or laughing in sun-splashed,   sea-dappled skies.
Free and fiery   they fly in their fury,
Then downward drift   a snow-storm of sunlight,
Clasping the earth   in cracking clear gold.

– tenth grade girl

Sapphic

A rhymeless, four-line stanza created by Sappho, a poetess who lived in ancient Greece. It uses the

Choriambus   – ⌣ ⌣ –
Amphibrach   ⌣ – ⌣
and Paeon II   ⌣ – ⌣ ⌣   or III ⌣ ⌣ – ⌣

– ⌣ ⌣ –   ⌣ – ⌣ ⌣ ⌣ – ⌣
– ⌣ ⌣ –   ⌣ – ⌣ ⌣ ⌣ – ⌣
– ⌣ ⌣ –   ⌣ – ⌣ ⌣ ⌣ – ⌣
– ⌣ ⌣ –

Glittering-throned,   undying Aphrodite,
Wile-weaving daughter   of Zeus I pray thee,
Tame not my soul   with heavy woe, dread mistress,
Nay, nor with anguish.

– Sappho

Long ere the day   when all the slaves are sleeping,
I in my boat   put out on the black water
Over us there   and under us the sunrise
Bursts on us blazing.

– Percy MacKaye

DESERT

Rush, wind-washed sand,   and sweep across the desert;
Mound to mountains,   crust to moveless crystal,
Always silent — a thousand years of wisdom,
Hidden forever.

– tenth grade girl

Limerick

A limerick is a humorous verse in which lines one, two and five rhyme, and lines three and four are a rhymed couplet. Lines one, two and five are iambic tetrameter, and lines three and four iambic trimeter.

MODERN COMPUTER

There was a computer named Zerk
Whose intricate head went berserk:
"I find that I need
A replacement. Indeed
I'll put all those humans to work."

– tenth grade girl

Haiku

A Japanese verse form consisting of three lines of five, seven, and five syllables respectively, and often referring to the weather and to a second, deeper meaning.

On this windless day
A butterfly is perching
On the temple bell.

– Japanese author

In what land is my
Little dragonfly hunter
Wandering tonight?

– Japanese author

The sun and flowers
All see themselves reflected
In butterflies' wings.

– a tenth grader

Triolet

A stanza of eight lines. It can be of any line length. Below, the capital letters mean the repetition of the entire line; the small letters indicate repetition of the rhyme only.

Modest is the triolet, **A**
Short and sweet, that's all, **B**
Fragile as a violet, **a**
Modest is the triolet. **A**
Winds that wander by, Oh let **a**
Fragrance on it fall. **b**
Modest is the triolet, **A**
Short and sweet. That's all. **B**

– Michael Lewis

Even though you are sure
  Music isn't eternal,
To me it will endure —
Even though you are sure
That it isn't the cure
  For all that's infernal,
Even though you are sure
That it isn't eternal.

– a tenth grader

The minutes pass away;
It is time we awaken.
Each hour we delay
The minutes pass away;
They cannot be retaken.
The minutes pass away
It is time we reawaken.

– a tenth grade girl

Sonnet

Fourteen lines of iambic pentameter.

Italian Sonnet: abba abba (octave) and six lines of various rhymes (sestet);

Shakespearian Sonnet: abab cdcd efef gg;

Spenserian Sonnet: abab bcbc cdcdee.

GUARDIAN

She walks the silent ocean of the stars
And wears the constellations as a crown;
The high gates of Infinity she bars

Lest mortals in bright heavens gaze should drown.
Where time is lost in Nothingness, where turns
The wheel of Fortune in majestic arc,
She rules the realm of every sun that burns
Its tiny candle in the boundless dark.

She gives the galaxies their distant glow,
And sees the world, the dying and reborn;
The age-old mysteries which men would know
She knows, but silent keeps; and men forlorn,
Gaze up into the deep and brilliant skies
And wonder why she smiles and shuts their eyes.

Melissa Merkling, who wrote this sonnet as a tenth-grade student in the Rudolf Steiner School of New York, is founder of the Star Meadow Kindergarten, a Waldorf kindergarten in Bridgewater, CT.

Spenserian Stanza

Eight lines iambic pentameter, then one of iambic hexameter.

When I ponder on life's mystery—	**a**
So much that we know not and never may—	**b**
I feel that in our clouded history	**a**
Something has been lost; and then I pray	**b**
That though man's present state may seem to say	**b**
Ours is a world of woe and pain and tears,	**c**
There will arise a brighter, cleaner day	**b**
When man shall use his soul for eyes and ears,	**c**
And all mankind shall know the Music of the Spheres	**c**

– an abbreviated Spenserian Stanza by a tenth-grade boy

Free Verse

Poetry based on the irregular rhythmic cadence of the recurrence of phrases and images rather than on the conventional use of meter. Rhyme may or may not be present.

SUN

Of course they worshipped you.
You are the god of the sky.
You sequin each morning's frost and dew
And paint the leaves and pebbles golden
In the evening.
You are the greatest artist of them all.
Your sun-shimmers are far more beautiful
Than Monet's, even in his prime,
Your skies more vibrant than van Gogh's,
Your sunsets far lovelier than any
Romantic painter in his most inspired moment.
It is towards you
That the plants reach
In their seasonal song of green and gold.
It is a longing for you
That makes the moths dance around flames,
And makes the people build their night fires
On the cold hills.
No sweet curve of the moon,
No sloping line of hills,
No graceful arch of birch,
No child's smile
Would be seen without your light.
You bring us rainbows,

And mornings,
And warmth,
And life.
You give without receiving,
And always will.
Above all else,
You
Deserve to be worshipped.
And so, great artist,
We will return your limitless love
With our own,
And smile our light upon you.

– eleventh grade girl

"Sun" was written by Kirsten Bergh while attending Hawthorne Valley School in Ghent, NY, a day before she was killed instantly in a car accident. As composed, the poem had no relationship to a school lesson or assignment. The poem is printed here with the kind permission of Kirsten's mother, Linda Bergh, 4315 Xerxes Ave., Minneapolis, MN 55410. It is taken from a volume of Kirsten's poems, *She Would Draw Flowers.*

The very best of such student work can be gathered in a yearly literary magazine. But it will only do its job if the teacher keeps it continually at heart and urges those with an especially promising poem or piece of prose to work it over still again and again. The student editors need to be encouraged and trained to base their judgments on positive, not negative grounds, and the teacher will do well to reserve the right of final veto even though she seldom or never uses it. Then the magazine can be held up with pride to the student body as an inspiration and a criterion for good work.

Each teacher will find his or her own way to let the music of poetry live in the memory, imagination, and moral fiber of the students. Then we can say of his or her pupils: *Let all such souls be trusted!*

Marianka Madey, eleventh grade, Hawthorne Valley School, Ghent, NY

Other Books of Interest

The Art and Science of Teaching Composition

Dorit Winter

This small but insightful book is an exploration of rich and stimulating methods for the teaching of English composition skills in Waldorf elementary schools. It offers writing exercises and examples. Compact, it is filled with wisdom all teachers will want to apply.

ISBN 978-1-888365-18-4
50 pages, 5.5 x 8.5 inches **$10.00**

Teaching Language Arts in the Waldorf School

Excerpts from *The Foundations of Waldorf Education* by Rudolf Steiner

Compiled by Roberto Trostli

This compendium aids Waldorf teachers by providing original comments from Rudolf Steiner on the teaching of language arts including: spelling, reading, composition writing, handwriting, left-handedness, literature, grammar, speech and recitation.

ISBN 978-1-888365-56-6
315 pages, 5.5 x 8.5 inches **$15.00**

The Power of Grammar

Anne Greer

Produced by the Research Institute for Waldorf Education and distributed by Waldorf Publications this book contains the proceedings of a recent colloquium where Anne Greer presented her novel approach to the subject. There are also contributions made by the illustrious participants.

Part 1: Background Research Chapters:
The Current Situation in NA Waldorf Schools
The Current Situations in NA Public Schools
What Does Rudolf Steiner Say about Teaching Grammar?
What's Wrong with What We're Already Doing?
The Linguisitic Revolution and the Teaching of Grammar
Mythrules
"Correcting" Student Errors
What's Useful in the New Approach to Grammar?
What Is Standard English?
What Might Work in a Waldorf High School

Part 2: Additional Contributions:
Meg Gorman: Bringing Traditional Grammar to Life
Wendy Bruneau: Using Image Grammar in the Classroom
Jason Gross: Seeing Grammar
Jason Gross: Serious Fun with Commas
Patrice Pinette: Grammar and Poetry
Jane Wulsin: "Study of Man"

ISBN 978-1-936367-74-0
172 pages, 7 x 10 inches **$24.00**

An English Manual

Dorothy Harrer

This classic has now been re-edited and updated. The author presents helpful suggestions for teaching English in grades 2 through 8. Speech exercises and notes from a composition workshop for teachers are also included.

ISBN 978-1-888365-48-1
134 pages, 5.5 x 8.5 inches **$14.00**

An English Grammar: The Language before Babel

Rudolf Schmidt

This book takes a poetic and in-depth look at sentence composition, parts of speech, sentence mood, and sentence movement. There are many wonderful examples taken from the works of masters of American and European literature.

ISBN 978-1-888365-15-3
139 pages, 8.5 x 11 inches **$16.00**

Word Mastery Primer For First and Second Graders

Hugh Renwick

The *Word Mastery Primer* is a wonderful resource to aid teachers in organizing word families and help them to create picture-filled stories. Words and phonemes are grouped artfully to make them memorable and delightful for children learning to read. This book serves also as a reader with imaginative short stories to help children practice the sound families they have learned. The author draws on a number of resources as well as his own considerable experience and creativity to build this short and comprehensive collection for teachers. The book has been used in manuscript form for teacher training in the Education Department at Antioch University, New England, for decades. This gem of a reading primer has helped hundreds of teachers in this most memorable approach to opening the world for children learning to put sounds together with letters.

ISBN 978-1-936367-87-0
128 pages, 8.5 x 11 inches **$16.00**

TO ORDER

Go to: www.waldorfpublications.org
Email: robin@waldorf-research.org
Call: 518-634-2222
Fax: 518-634-2597

Printed in Great Britain
by Amazon